2]

Stretching the Eyes' Distance...

Reflections on the Chesapeake Bay

by

Barclay Sheaks

Bartley Sheaks

Barclay Sheaks '77

Barclay Sheaks approaches his summation of the Bay in the way in which he excels — by evoking from his own unique visual and verbal imagery a crow's nest of mood and perception to view the ever-changing, never-changing wonder of his Chesapeake Bay.

Humans seek in their lives patterns of balance, employing basic cycles of stability complemented by the inspiration of the unpredictable. Here the Chesapeake Bay becomes the persona of this quixotic constancy. Its great appeal for Sheaks rests in his observation of the primary core of equilibrium achieved by its uniquely embellished, yet repeated patterns, whether they be the return flight of the osprey, the ebb and flow of the tide, or the rhythm of the oyster tongers.

It is exhilarating to be an observer always on the eve of wonder, braced by underlying pattern, and thus freed to appreciate surface variations. Such is the nature of renascence in the life cycles of the Bay. In this continuum each season holds the promise of the next in a pattern of renewal from which we watchers are sustained with hope and optimism. Not only has Barclay Sheaks offered us many pictorial angles from which to view this becoming, he has also drafted a compact wealth of word-beams to gladden our inward eye.

— *Nancy Gotwald Harris, Editor*

it was spring— and a beginning

Genesis I — A Beginning

It was a wild and lonely place
she found for her nest —
        the first one —
a wind shaped hollow
just above the tide line
where the flotsam rests from the storm;
a circle of shells the seabird made
        to mark her space.

        The eggs came
frail from her slender body;
close on the earth she placed them
        to quicken in the sun.
They lay in her magic ring
        by the bay's edge,
like old pebbles, or sea cast stones.
But they were new — it was spring —
        and a beginning.

Barclay Sheaks '80

Umbra

I walk alone
in the morning early
where the shore can go no further
into sand and foam.
The light just off the beach
above the breakers' sound
decides what sort of day
it will become,
and I recall other rainy days
when figures ran free
in an old landscape
on the dawn's dark side.

Up The Bay In The Rain

Today the boat holds to the waves
in a lover's reluctant parting.
Near the shore an osprey startled
        by the motor's sound
launches upward from its buoy
        in wild dark pattern.
She returns after our passing,
following an old course,
turning to land into the wind
        as always.

Spring On The Chesapeake

Sailors study channel and chart,
check fittings and shroud,
    polish brass.
Watermen make ready
with new rope and floats,
    speculating the season.
The marina drums with the sound
of engine and winch;
dry hulls on the railway
feel the scraper's bite
    as old coatings peel.
On their own flood the bluefish arrive—
    gull traced,
pursued by feathered lure.
Crabs move into the eelgrass—
sliding shadows on the tide.
The marsh seeps green
    as winter ebbs,
and the Chesapeake blossoms
with white boat shapes
    and bright spinnakers.

Big Marsh

There is a marsh that starts at Wachapreague
and runs down the shore to Quinby
      and beyond,
stretching the eyes' distance to the ocean,
a grass selvage that keeps the edge of land.
If you should come upon it suddenly
      in any season,
especially if taken
in equal measure with the sky,
that vision blooms like cold fire —
      indelible memory.

across bright summer

Finding Tangier For The First Time
(Notes From A Bay Journal)

Morning

Plowing the soft mist of daybreak
we head north from Windmill Point—
      destination—Tangier.
Keeping the compass close
we seek another world on a sunless day.

Riding the swell's ridge in a following sea,
the propeller sometimes catches air
and blows foam along the wake—
a white trail on the grey and green.

Mid-day

Aware of the liquid emptiness
      and summer heat,
we argue over the course setting
      and the engine speed,
thinking we've outrun the chart.
The depth gauge shows only echoes.

A pale shadow drifts on the sky's edge,
      a web of boat masts
topped by a single church spire.
      Tangier at last.

Our boat threads the erratic space of markers,
      through the land's arm
where stilted houses stand tip-toe,
clean shapes that look inward from the sea.
      We are anchored
in their pattern of reflection.

Evening

Never again for this place
will there be this vision—
first blood of discovery.
Its bright image was held
in a dark hand's liquid palm
      for a moment.
Now the world is smaller,
reduced to outlined recollections.
      It is over.

A boat called the *Tangier Princess* is docking.
The evening tide runs strong to the south
      toward Cape Charles.

Summer Panorama

As life moves in, up and out
across the Bay,
summer surfaces;
green moves back from shore
to tended field
and beyond —
leaf into blossom.

Crab pots in ragged line
follow the season's cycle
from channel's depth to tidal flat.
Workboats crowd the morning;
haulseines and gill nets
float the evening tide.

Forests of boat masts
in marinas like those at Annapolis,
Solomons, Crisfield and Poquoson
sprout rigging and sail —
eager children in pursuit of the wind.

Doors swing back,
shutters open on new vistas
as the summer residents return,
weary from city and winter.
Tourists, weekenders and sunseekers —
they come with the season,
drawn by thoughts of bright days
and slow warm nights
filled with feasting by the shore.

Pulling and raking,
reaching and netting,
clammers comb the shoals;
crabbers probe tidepools.
Children chase minnows
with sticks and laughter;
lovers find secret islands.

The sun's heat clouds the water
as summer moves on the Bay.

Tide Pool

When the tide recedes
the water relinquishes the land
reluctantly.
A barely perceptible retreat,
it resists the moon's magnetic pull,
until finally
tide joins the current's race.
A few outposts do not surrender;
those tidepools stand
reflecting the sky,
small echoes of the sea
remaining.

Eastern Shore Watermen

They look about the same as any laborer,
at first.
If you're use to watching people,
you notice their bony hips
hitch up a little higher when they walk
from holding the oyster tongs;
their hands get knobby
and old
before reaching twenty
from working on the cold water
in winter.
It's the way they talk
that makes them different,
beautiful like poetry.
You'd take their words and use them
if you could,
stringing them together for your own.
But you couldn't make it yaw
like they do,
profanely gentle,
riding the curses to the story's end,
cutting it off just so,
gesturing to make the meaning clear.
They don't seem much different
at first,
'till you hear them speak.

Headin' Up Route 13

Take it from me,
if you're headin' north up route 13
on the eastern shore
and you turn left or right
on any sideroad,
more or less
you'll come to the water,
Bay on the left, ocean on the right.
The same is true if you're movin' south,
'cept
the water you see is just the opposite
of that you'd come to
if you're goin' the other way.
Do it at Painter, Exmore or Birdsnest,
anywhere the roads cross.
You might pass
churches and store, empty houses,
cropper's shacks,
migrant workers,
whites, blacks, chickens and children,
or dogs sleepin' in the sun,
big farm mansions that step up and down
as they were added on to,
with dead cars propped up
on cinder blocks.
The paved road might turn
to rutted tracks that lead back
along hedgerows to the marsh's edge,
but when it stops, finally,
take it from me,
you'll be at the water,
more or less.

Summer Hour

Thunderheads roll sullen
across bright summer.
Winds agitate the Bay
a textured blue,
dark where it meets the sky,
light where sun patches fall.
Into the sheltering land's arm
the small boat lies anchored —
a white arrow moored into the wind,
acknowledging the wave swells.
The hull's sanctuary is a cradle for lovers.
Safe they swim naked,
knowing salty skin
and the liquid feel of floating free
in a summer hour.

the slant on slant of autumn wind and sun

Barclay Sheaks '77

Now October

The slant on slant of autumn wind and sun
upon the marsh,
beginning from the bay in patterned waves
moves daily down each stem of grass
in slender browning death.

The hunter cat moves quicker now,
a dark shadow
following the vanished edge of summer.

None escaping,
each we feel time's sudden piercing
and know this season with remorse.

Night Journey

Outward I turn from the land world
of dark, flat cornfields
scarred by the long black symmetry
of night and highway,
downward towards the eastern shore
and the sea,
on roads like cowpaths.
The real world falls away in chunks,
separating a piece at a time
with each bridge passed
until unencumbered
the island and I meet—
two islands floating free—
somewhere between the sky,
the water and the night.

Autumn Beach From A Distance

Light sky down under,
shot with autumn thunder,
reflects in puddled road.
Storm threats test the tern's wings,
fletched over with wonder.

Down the beach,
dunehigh and nestled,
followed by tracks
not yet returning,
two lovers know first touches,
aware of grass viewed skyward
with firm sand under.

Boys with new hunting caps
shoot sea birds,
watching them—blood feathered—
falling into the surf,
pink rising from under,
knowing the sounds of a different thunder.

still in the marsh and cold

Snow Geese

Out of the refuge and the night
they come,
blown like torn paper.
White on the wind,
through the sky fissures
they ride the flow of halting cry,
matching their downward flight
to the sounds
of magnum tens and twelves.
Fire flashes in the marsh.
White on white and crimson
they fall,
smaller now in death,
packages of twisted rag,
still in the marsh and cold.

Winter Marsh

The marsh moves back
stretching cleanly away
like a carefully drawn breath
from the barrier beach,
wounded from autumn storms,
covered with old picnics
and shiny paths
where the grass is bent
from the wind.
A small boat passes
far out.

Wintry Day

The faded dune grass blooms now
frosted bronze and silver against the pines.
Only the hawk — quick death flying —
moves with confidence,
sliding his shadow like a knife
along the edge of winter.

Chincoteague — Frozen In
(Winter of '77)

Chincoteague frozen in,
ice piled up in the channel,
reaching out into the ocean beyond vision,
deeper than memory,
cold extended past generations of stories.

Wild fowl, geese and brant,
foiled by glacial curtain,
drop with hunger from the sky
into house yards,
and feed by doorsteps with dogs
who watch silently,
bewildered.

Boats lie solid as the earth,
still,
their riggings white bones in the sunlight.
Tides no longer rise.
Watermen, shore-bound, wait
like pardoned prisoners
on the last day,
tinkering with their gear,
while ice wounds the soft
white sides of their boats
as a sharp knife cuts flesh.
They spend the last of their money
on beer in a dockside tavern
biding the thaw
that does not come.

Barkley Shanks '73

comes a stillness.....

Comes A Stillness

The Bay is tired,
exhausted from winter.
No whisper now—
the ragged marsh rattles
sharp in the wind.
Shores lie gutted,
markers and poles askew;
gull flock inland,
white patterns that wait
the farmer's furrow.

Comes a stillness;
then the tide,
another season rises
as it flows.